Makayla's Birthday Money!

Work with Money

Josiah Byrd

ROSEN
COMMON CORE MATH
READERS

Rosen
Classroom™

New York

Published in 2015 by The Rosen Publishing Group, Inc.
29 East 21st Street, New York, NY 10010

Book Design: Mickey Harmon

Photo Credits: Cover, p. 5 Dragon Images/Shutterstock.com; p. 7 Jamie Grill/Getty Images; pp. 9, 11 (dollar bill) Garsya/
Shutterstock.com; pp. 9, 11, 15, 17, 19, 21 (wood) 9peaks/Shutterstock.com; p. 11 (5 dollar bill) Robynrg/
Shutterstock.com; p. 13 (table) Maglara/Shutterstock.com; p. 13 (money) Calvste/Shutterstock.com; p. 14 rangizzz/
Shutterstock.com; pp. 15, 17, 19, 21 (coins) Asaf Eliason/Shutterstock.com; p. 16 cjorgens/Shutterstock.com;
p. 18 kanate/Shutterstock.com; p. 21 (bookstore) 06photo/Shutterstock.com; p. 22 martellostudio/Shutterstock.com.

Library of Congress Cataloging-in-Publication Data

Byrd, Josiah, author.
 Makayla's birthday money! : work with money / Josiah Byrd.
    pages cm. — (Math masters. Measurement and data)
 Includes index.
 ISBN 978-1-4777-4822-0 (pbk.)
 ISBN 978-1-4777-4823-7 (6-pack)
 ISBN 978-1-4777-6407-7 (library binding)
 1. Arithmetic—Juvenile literature. 2. Money—Juvenile literature. I. Title.
 QA115.B99 2015
 513—dc23
                              2013047297

Manufactured in the United States of America

CPSIA Compliance Information: Batch #WS15RC: For further information contact Rosen Publishing, New York, New York at 1-800-237-9932.

Contents

A Birthday Party

Yesterday was Makayla's birthday! She turned 8 years old. Makayla had a big birthday party, and her whole family came to her house to **celebrate**.

Makayla's grandma gave her a colorful birthday card with some money inside. Makayla's mom told her she could spend some of her birthday money at the store. She also said Makayla should save some of her birthday money. Then, she'll have money to spend later, too.

Makayla is learning about money in her math class at school.

Adding with Dollars

Makayla counted the money in the birthday card from her grandma. The money looked like pieces of paper. They're called bills. Each bill had a 1 written on it, which means it's **worth** 1 dollar.

Makayla learned in school that dollars can be written using a special sign called the dollar sign. If Makayla wanted to use the dollar sign to show 1 dollar, she would write $1.

1 dollar = $1

The dollar sign is a kind of symbol. It's a shape that stands for something else.

Makayla's grandma gave her 5 dollars for her birthday. Then, Makayla found 2 more dollars in a birthday card from her aunt. How many dollars does Makayla have altogether?

She can count the dollar bills to find out, or use addition. By adding 5 dollars and 2 dollars, Makayla sees that she has 7 dollars altogether. Using the dollar sign, she can write that amount as $7.

$$\begin{array}{r} \$5 \\ +\ \$2 \\ \hline \$7 \end{array}$$

Math problems with dollars are just like any other kind of math problem. You just have to remember to use the dollar sign!

Makayla also got some birthday money from her mom. Her mom gave her 1 bill with the number 5 on it. She explained to Makayla that this bill is worth 5 dollars. It's the same as having five $1 bills, which is what Makayla's grandma gave her.

If Makayla adds the birthday money from her mom and grandma, how much will she have altogether? She will have 10 dollars, or $10.

 +

Makayla knows she can show $10 using different **combinations** of bills. She can use ten $1 bills, two $5 bills, or one $10 bill.

What Are Cents?

Makayla's brother gave her money for her birthday, too. The money he gave her is in the form of little, round pieces of **metal**. These are called coins.

One kind of coin is called a penny, and it's worth much less than 1 dollar. In fact, it takes 100 pennies to equal 1 dollar. A penny is worth 1 cent, which can be written as 1¢ when you use the cent symbol.

1 cent = 1¢
100 cents = $1

There are 100 cents in every dollar. That's a lot of pennies!

Pennies and Nickels

Makayla had 6 pennies in her hand, and she put 1 in her piggy bank to save for later. How many cents does she have left? Makayla can subtract 1 cent from 6 cents to find the answer. She can see that she has 5 cents, or 5¢.

Makayla learned that there's 1 coin equal to 5 cents. It's called a nickel.

Makayla's piggy bank is full of many different kinds of coins!

6¢
− 1¢
――――
5¢

At the Toy Store

A dime is another kind of coin. It's worth 10 pennies, or 10 cents. Makayla bought a doll at the toy store with some of her birthday money. She got 2 dimes back from the woman who works there.

By skip counting, Makayla can see that 2 dimes are the same as 20 cents. How many nickels would it take to make 20 cents?

10¢ + 10¢ = 20¢

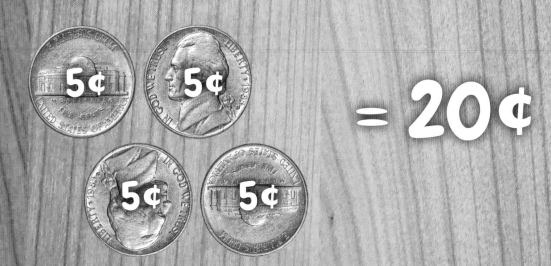 = 20¢

5¢ + 5¢ + 5¢ + 5¢ = 20¢

Makayla can count by 5s to see that 4 nickels make 20 cents.

Buying a Book

Makayla also wanted to buy a book with some of her birthday money, but she needed 1 more dollar. Makayla's mom showed her how to make a dollar using another kind of coin in her piggy bank. It's called a quarter. 1 quarter is the same as 25 cents.

Makayla had 3 quarters in her piggy bank, and her mom gave her 1 more. Does Makayla have enough money to buy the book?

25¢ + 25¢ + 25¢ + 25¢ = 100¢ = $1

Makayla added the 4 quarters and saw that they're worth 100 cents, or 1 dollar. She had enough money for the book!

After Makayla bought her book, she got coins back from the man who works at the bookstore. He gave her 2 quarters, 1 dime, and 1 nickel. How much money did Makayla get back altogether?

Makayla knows 1 quarter is worth 25 cents, so 2 quarters are worth 50 cents. She also knows 1 dime is worth 10 cents, and 1 nickel is worth 5 cents. How much is that worth altogether?

$$25¢ + 25¢ + 10¢ + 5¢ = ?¢$$

25¢ + 10¢ + 5¢ = ?¢

25¢

Makayla saw many books she'd like to buy in the bookstore. She's going to save her money to buy another book there soon!

A Super Saver!

Makayla felt very thankful for all her birthday presents. She liked being able to spend her birthday money on some special things, such as a doll and a book. She also put some of the money back in her piggy bank to save for later. Saving money is very important. It allows you to have money for things you need and want at a later time.

Makayla is learning how to be a good saver!

Glossary

celebrate (SEH-luh-brayt) To do special things for a holiday or other important day.

combination (kahm-buh-NAY-shun) A joining of different parts.

metal (MEH-tuhl) Shiny and hard matter.

worth (WUHRTH) Equal in value to.

Index

Due to the changing nature of Internet links, The Rosen Publishing Group, Inc., has developed an online list of websites related to the subject of this book. This site is updated regularly. Please use this link to access the list: **www.powerkidslinks.com/mm/mad/mbm**